AUTHENTICALLY
SOCIAL

BREAK THROUGH BY BEING YOU!

COREY PERLMAN

This book is dedicated to the legacy of my mom, Janet Perlman. She modeled what it looks like to live an authentic life. She was unapologetically herself and loved deeply and unconditionally. The impact she left on me, my brother, my children, and her beloved clients will live on for generations to come.

Thank you for everything, mom, I love you.

ACKNOWLEDGMENTS

I am deeply grateful for the incredible support and inspiration I received throughout the creation of *Authentically Social*. This journey was made possible by the generosity, encouragement, and expertise of so many remarkable individuals.

Jessica Perlman, thank you for being my partner in life and business. This book would have remained a fleeting thought in my head without your grit and determination to keep the music from dying inside me. I love you.

Talia and Milo, thank you for giving me the space and breathing room to write. I never liked being apart from you guys, but I felt your love and support while dad was away.

Dad and Kate, thank you for always being in my corner. You fill me up with unconditional love and give me the confidence to go out and live my dreams.

Jaime, my brotha—thank you for bringing joy to my life. You remind me that the true joy in life happens in the memories we create. I look forward to many more fun times with you and the family.

Julie Meacham and Jess Pettitt, the red pen mafia! Thank you for your attention to detail and for working so hard to avoid revealing my bad grammar habits—specifically my improper use of commas.

Jenn Nagy, you are a super-talented graphic designer, and I feel so fortunate that I get to show your work off to the world. Thank you for your commitment to me and our team!

Halina Miller, thank you for the invaluable gift of keeping us organized and on schedule. This book would have never gotten to the finish line without your talent for "nicely nagging."

To Carla and Courtney, thank you for all the hard work you have done with our clients over the years that helped to create some of the great success stories outlined in this book.

Desi Lazzara, thank you for sifting through so much content to find the gold amongst the dirt.

Gwyn Flowers, thank you for compiling all the pieces and parts of this manuscript into one beautiful work of art.

To Bethany Brown and The Cadence Group, thank you for your help with publishing and distribution.

Finally, thank you to all our clients for trusting us with your digital brand and marketing. We do not take it for granted and are forever grateful for your business and loyalty.

AUTHENTICALLY SOCIAL PRINCIPLES

INTRODUCTION

Social media has revolutionized the way businesses engage with their audiences. Gone are the days of one-sided marketing campaigns. Today, customers demand more from the brands they choose to support. They seek authenticity – a genuine human connection that transcends the impersonal facade of corporate messaging.

Welcome to *Authentically Social: Breakthrough by Being You!*

In this book, we will embark on a journey to explore the transformative impact of authenticity on businesses in the dynamic realm of social media.

In an era where trust is paramount—and the digital landscape is overflowing with noise—authenticity has emerged as the secret ingredient that sets exceptional businesses apart from the rest. It goes beyond polished marketing strategies and scripted interactions. It's about fostering real, meaningful connections with customers, team members, and the broader community.

Throughout these pages, we will explore the essence of authenticity on social media—what it means, why it matters, and how it shapes the future of successful businesses. Drawing from over a decade of agency experience and real-world client examples, we will uncover the strategies employed by industry leaders who have harnessed the power of authenticity to build loyal followers.

We will discover how authenticity encourages businesses to showcase their humanity—the faces, voices, and stories that breathe life into their brands. Moreover, we will uncover the extraordinary potential for businesses to foster a sense of belonging. Where customers become more than consumers; they become cherished members of a community.

As we navigate the complexities of social media authenticity, challenges and fears that businesses might encounter on this path less traveled will be addressed. From navigating the fine line between personal and professional to managing potential risks, you will be equipped with insights to confidently navigate the digital landscape.

The digital revolution has placed tremendous power in the hands of businesses, enabling them to reach audiences far and wide. But with this power comes an immense responsibility—a responsibility to use these platforms to connect, uplift, and inspire. The authenticity we foster on social media will help us build trust and credibility with our audience and build a foundation for enduring relationships.

When did social media lose its authenticity?

I've pondered this question over the past few years and believe the answer lies in the way most businesses approach their overall digital strategy. Instead of putting human connection at the forefront of their digital strategy, they took an artificial approach with automation and curated content from outside sources.

X (the social media site formerly known as Twitter) is my favorite example of this massive swing. When Twitter first launched, it was a platform of people connecting with people. Today, it is dominated by bots, automated direct messages, and pre-populated content. There is very little authenticity about it anymore. And thus, it has lost its luster. This is happening on all social platforms. The key word that has been lost on all of these sites is...**social.**

So...let's talk about you and your business. **If I check out your digital footprint, what will I see?** Is it made up of engaging content worthy of your customers and prospects? Or is it a sea of curated content with no connection to your identity? Would you consider yourself authentically social?

If your social media looks like a billboard or brochure—you're doing it wrong.

People want to connect with people. And so, no matter the size of your business or industry, the more transparent, personal, and authentic your brand, the better the engagement.

That sounds easy enough, but how do you do it both consistently and efficiently?

I've taken 15+ years of experience and knowledge and boiled it down to **20 Authentic Principles** that have produced real results for our clients.

Did I say results?!?

Results might as well be a four-letter-word in the world of social media. It's been a point of contention ever since Facebook went from college connections to exploding profits.

Results can mean many different things to many people. Some monitor likes, comments, emojis, shares, and other engagement metrics, while others measure results in website clicks, email opt-ins, phone calls, and office visits. Then, there are those who believe the only metric that matters is the bottom line. All of these are important indicators of whether your social media efforts are working and should all be taken into account when measuring success.

I believe the results we should all strive for are building trust and strengthening credibility. If someone trusts us and believes we are the authority on a given topic, they will not only buy from us but also refer others to us. These loyal followers become our advocates, our champions, and our most powerful sales force. And that, my friends, is the holy grail of social media. That's how I measure success.

How do we do this? It's actually quite simple. We stop looking at our social media as a sales tool and start looking at it as a relationship-building tool. It's not advertising. It's not a billboard or 30-second advertisement. You've chosen to participate in social media—the keyword being *social*. It's time to treat it that way. We need to get more personal, add more value, and create more meaningful conversations.

I'm going to show you how to do it in this book.

Let's go!

Feedback

Yes, I want to hear your feedback on this book, as I really want to make you and your business better at social media. I believe this book will. I'd be honored if you'd share your positive experience on Amazon or wherever you bought my book. As you'll learn in *Authentically Social*, people are more motivated to give feedback when they're unhappy rather than happy. Therefore, I'm taking my own advice to be proactive and asking you for your authentic review if you find this book helpful to you and your business. Likewise, if you did not find this book helpful, relevant, or valuable, I would also like to hear from you. I have created a specific site for this called MySpace.com. Feel free to post it there and await a response from a guy named Tom. If you get that joke, you also chatted on AIM, emailed through Hotmail, and navigated via Netscape. You're my people!

Thank You.

I know there's an abundance of information out there on the topic of social media, yet you've given me your valuable time and attention. I appreciate you doing so—and I understand the gravity of its impact. If you should finish this book and still have questions, please don't hesitate to reach out. My email is corey@impactsocialmedia.com, or connect with me at LinkedIn. com/in/CoreyPerlman. I would love to stay in touch with you, and I hope you will also stay in touch with me.

How each chapter of the book is laid out

- **The Principle.** Here, I will share one of the rules that our agency has come to live by while serving our clients over the last decade. These rules drive engagement, increase leads, and keep our clients "top of mind" with their audience.

- **The Mantra.** This is the "sticky note" phrase that hopefully lives by your computer, and reminds you to apply the principle that resonates the most with you and your business.

- **A Success Story.** Each chapter has at least one story from an organization, business or individual that put the principle into action and saw tangible results.

- **How to Take Action.** Information is meaningless unless it leads to action. Each chapter will include clear action steps that are easy to implement and will positively impact your business.

SECTION ONE

Strategy

Over the years, I've watched a lot of time, money and resources get wasted on the wrong platforms and toward the wrong audiences. As the saying goes, the train was doomed before it ever left the station. This first section is dedicated to ensuring this doesn't happen to you or your business. Even if you are well established on social media, this is a great opportunity to pause and reflect on how you're approaching your social media marketing. How should you appear on social media? Which platforms should you prioritize? How are you proactively connecting with your target audience? These are just some of the questions you'll answer as you work through section one and start to take your digital marketing in a new and different direction.

Be Yourself, Everyone Else Is Taken

MANTRA
My digital brand should be an authentic reflection of me.

O ver the last decade of owning a social media agency, one thing has become abundantly clear: **people want to engage with and do business with** *people*. Your products or services may be what drives people to you, but it is the way you present yourself and your ideas that will build trust and inevitably earn their business.

When considering what authentically social means for you and your brand, it's important to do some self-evaluating and self-reflection of what it is that makes you who you really are. As Simon Sinek so famously said, "Find your why." What inspires who you are and the work you do? What are the qualities within yourself that feel the most honest and truthful to you? The answers should be at the heart of your social media strategy.

We've all run across social media profiles that look or feel inauthentic. Have you ever caught yourself needing to act a certain way or even portray a false narrative for one reason or another? We know how disingenuous that feels, and the goal should be to present your full, authentic self. Nothing will resonate better with people, potential customers, than you being you. Find your strengths, and then double down on them. Be energetic, silly, serious, funny, or whatever is most authentic to you and your business.

Take some time to reflect on the qualities that make you genuinely authentic. Try writing some of these qualities down on sticky notes and placing them where you can see them often. Once you feel confident in your authentic self, you'll have no problem being the real you on social media.

I truly believe that when you put authenticity at the core of your social media, you'll be more relatable, trustworthy, and credible to your audience. This is how we create long-term relationships that will keep your business growing for years to come.

When Jennifer got her dream job as CEO of a large training and development company, she called me to share the exciting news. After a few minutes of celebrating, we got down to business. She needed help with her LinkedIn profile, as she didn't believe her engagement (likes, comments, shares) met the high standards of her new position. She wanted a social media makeover, and she wanted it fast! She was also insistent that she remain hidden behind the scenes. As instructed, we set off posting articles, white papers, and other corporate content that we received from her marketing department. It looked perfectly curated … professionally written … and sad. It looked sad because no one was engaging with her or her content. After a month of social media silence from her audience, Jennifer was open to trying something different.

We discovered that Jennifer was great on camera and a fantastic interviewer. With a little convincing, we helped her launch a podcast where she interviewed other female executives about the challenges and opportunities they faced in the marketplace. Jennifer's passion, enthusiasm, and humor naturally came through as she engaged in these conversations. She made her guests feel at ease and brought out great value in every episode. She got more engagement on this podcast series than anything else she had ever posted. Friends, colleagues, and prospects all chimed in to share their excitement. Her newly engaged followers even shared episodes on their profiles, which expanded her reach exponentially. Jennifer's personal brand took off and, along with it, the business brand was amplified as well. She became a true believer that people enjoyed being connected to her … not just her content.

1. Take a look at this list of character traits:

CHARACTER TRAITS

Funny	Enthusiastic	Witty	Passionate
Genuine	Outgoing	Spontaneous	Quick-Thinking
Detail-Oriented	Adventurous	Silly	Professional
Introverted	Extroverted	Intellectual	High-Energy

2. Highlight the ones that resonate most with you and your personality.

3. I left four blank so you can add your own traits.

4. Keep these words close to you, and remind yourself to let them shine through when you're creating content on social media.

Beware the Shiny Penny Syndrome

MANTRA

Don't be a jack of all social media sites, master of none.

As I write this book, there's a war and potential cage fight being waged between Elon Musk and Mark Zuckerberg. Mark has chosen a time when X seems weak and has brought forth a competitor to take down one of its rivals. That's right, Threads is the latest social media flavor of the month and has the world wondering if this will be one of the major platforms of the future or face a similar fate as the late Google+ (may it rest in peace). Only time will tell. My advice to you is the same advice I give each time a new and shiny social media site enters the battlefield. Be patient. All too often, social media sites make headlines with impressive early adoption rates, only to peter out a few months later. My advice to most businesses is to give it time and see if usage continues to grow. Pay attention to demographics and see if your target audience starts to spend significant time on the new platform. It wasn't long ago when people spent lots of time and resources building a following on Google+ only to watch it fade away into the internet abyss.

I believe you should have a top three social media priority list at all times. If Threads (or any other social media site that comes along) becomes worthy of replacing one of your top three, then that might be a time to reevaluate. When you add another social media site to your priority list, it always comes at the expense of energy and resources from your prioritized top three. Focus on a few and do them really well. Avoid the Shiny Penny Syndrome.

Considerations you should take into account before picking up the Shiny Penny:

- Would this platform benefit my brand/business?
- Does this platform align with my brand/business?
- Would participating on this platform compromise my voice and values?
- Am I joining this platform only because everyone else is?
- What loses my attention if I spend more time here?

Choose three social platforms to focus on and eliminate the rest.

Besides owning a digital marketing agency, I also do keynote presentations for companies and associations on how to see better results by being Authentically Social. In those 10 years, I've never had a heckler … but a talk in North Dakota was as close as I'd like to come.

I spoke to a group of executives out of Bismarck, and a question came up from the audience about TikTok. At the time of this speech, TikTok was the new shiny penny, and media pundits were adding fuel to the fire by talking about it daily. As I answered a lady's question, an older gentleman on the other side of the room slammed his hands on the table and shoved the hotel pad and paper right to the floor. It was so loud that it startled me and the rest of the room.

I actually didn't know what to say, so I just looked at the audience for guidance … or the nearest exit.

He collected himself and began to speak, "I'm sorry, Corey. I didn't mean to interrupt or freak everyone out. I'm just frustrated."

"I can see that," I managed to say as I finally figured out how to talk again. "Why are you frustrated?"

"I can't keep up. Just when I feel like I have a handle on Facebook, Instagram, LinkedIn, along comes Snap Chatty and Tikkity Tok (I think he knew the names—this was just for effect), and I'm tired of it!"

I felt his pain. Not only had I heard this complaint from countless others, I've felt it! There are just too many to keep up with, and I have the added pressure of trying to stay relevant in an ever-changing industry. It can be overwhelming.

"I hear you," I said back to him. "What type of business are you in?"

This next part is too hard for me to even make up. It gave the whole audience the biggest laugh of the day.

The frustrated gentleman said, "I sell timeshares to retirees."

Once again, I was speechless. As was the audience … except for a few people's hands hitting their foreheads.

With what felt like minutes, we just stared at each other. I knew he was processing what he just said.

"Do I even need to worry about TikTok?" he asked.

In unison, the entire audience screamed out, "NOOOOOOO!" It was obvious to everyone else that this man's target audience is unlikely to be on TikTok.

His energy changed. "Oh, good," he said calmly.

His eyebrow furrowed again, "What about Snapchat?"

"Not for about 50 years, my friend," I said.

He smiled, picked up his notepad, and settled in for the rest of the talk.

Although funny and outrageous, how many of us have truly looked at our audience demographics BEFORE determining where to put our energy and efforts on social media? Ask yourself not only whether you should be on a particular platform but also which sites should take priority AND the majority of your attention.

It's okay to be strategically not *there*.

Here is how to determine which platforms are best for you:

1. Who's your target audience? I know that for many of us, we cast a wide net, but the 80/20 rule should apply. Know where the bulk of your business comes from. Specifically, whose attention do you need to grab? Are they 30-40? Mostly women? Entrepreneurs? Salespeople at mid-size companies? Knowing the right target demographic for your product is key.

2. Perform a quick Google search using "Social Media Demographics" and the current year. In a few short minutes, you'll get an idea of which platforms your customers use the most.

3. Once you've determined who your audience is and which platforms they frequent most, build your social media strategy around those platforms and leave the rest behind.

Take Pride in Your Profiles

MANTRA

i'm as proud of my online brand as i am my products or services.

I'm going to go out on a limb and assume you make exceptional products or provide extraordinary service. If I walked into your showroom, listened in on a meeting, or explored your inventory, I'd likely be impressed. But what if I Googled you, stumbled upon your website, or visited your social media profiles? Would these also impress me? Or would I find a disconnect between your offline and online brand?

It doesn't matter if you work within a large company or are an army of one—don't accept mediocrity when it comes to your online brand. In today's digital world, an online touchpoint may act as your first impression. And like all first impressions, it's imperative that you make it a good one.

When I do a digital audit of a personal or business brand, here are five things that I look for:

1. Brand consistency across all platforms. This includes colors, fonts, images, etc.

2. Up-to-date information. I want to be sure what I'm reading or watching is current and not from years past. Old information could create doubts about the status or viability of your business.

3. Content consistency. This can be accomplished in a few ways: daily social media posts, weekly blog articles, or monthly videos. It's important for me to see that you or your company are doing great things and that you are ready to serve when your customers are ready to buy.

4. Positive sentiment. This is a big one. On each platform I visit, I check if the overall sentiment is positive or negative. If positive reviews or testimonials are lacking, I recommend asking happy customers to post to those profiles.

5. Profiles that are dormant. Did an ambitious intern come in and create a Snapchat profile that's never been used? Unmanaged or unused profiles should be deleted or brought back to life. Dormant profiles should not be left to sit without consistent posts and a plan to build a following.

A quality brand might take different shapes and forms depending on the industry. For example, a law firm would want to exhibit consistent professionalism across all platforms and have the same quality and consistency with individual LinkedIn profiles for those who work within the firm. Additionally, a restaurant will want to ensure that its online profiles match the style and concept of its dining area. There should be no separation between an offline and online brand. They should act as one—a consistent and cohesive representation of who you are, what you do, and how you serve others.

Our agency has had some really cool clients over the years. One of my personal favorites was a group of Harley-Davidson dealerships across the Midwest. I took my team to one of the dealerships, and as we toured the showroom, it took our collective breath away. Each motorcycle was more impressive than the next – quality and craftsmanship unmatched by anything we'd ever seen. After our tour, we gathered in their boardroom to discuss our taking over their digital marketing. I watched as my team's excitement turned to disbelief as we looked at their social media profiles. We scrolled through blurry photos, inconsistent fonts, dated logos, and a hodgepodge of colors that had nothing to do with their brand. The Harley-Davidson team could clearly see how underwhelmed we were at the state of their digital profiles. "You have your work cut out for you!" one of the owners said.

We worked on establishing consistent fonts, colors, and other design elements for the dealerships. Their sales manager sent us hundreds of recently taken professional photos of their new inventory. And with a little nudging, we encouraged them to hire a professional videographer to do a virtual tour of the dealerships. We now had the necessary elements to redesign their profiles to match the beautiful motorcycles they so proudly displayed in their showroom. For the first time ever, there was no disconnect between the online and offline world. No matter where a prospect stumbled upon them, the Harley-Davidson team could be proud of their first impression.

TAKE ACTION

Set a timer for 15 minutes and pretend you're a busy prospect determining whether to do business with you or not. Google your name or the name of your business. Scan the results and click on a few links on the first page. When the 15 minutes are up, answer these questions:

- Are you impressed by what you see?

- Do you get a positive first impression no matter which profile you click on?

- Is it clear what you do and who you serve?

- Do you have any pages or profiles that are being unmanaged?

- Is your content helpful? Do you feel like you're adequately serving your audience?

- Is there negative sentiment on any of your profiles or directories?

- Is there a low number of followers or lack of engagement on any profiles?

You should end up with a checklist when you complete this exercise. Commit to addressing these issues and ensure that no matter where someone starts, they always start with a great first impression.

BONUS ACTION: Give a Little Love to Your LinkedIn

Your LinkedIn profile is an easy place for people to check you out before meeting or doing business with you. Here are a few ways to make sure you are laying the foundation to leave a great first impression.

- **Update your profile photo.** Be sure your photo is current and relevant to now.

- **The Background Photo.** The background photo is often overlooked on your LinkedIn profile. It's a great opportunity for you to visually demonstrate who you are and what you do.

- **Tagline.** Three to five words that explain exactly what you do. LinkedIn is often used as a search engine, and the words in your tagline often dictate where and when you show up in a search.

- **Professional Summary.** Unless you're looking for a job, your professional summary should not be a bio. It should be a benefit-rich summary of how you help people.

- **Recommendations.** When I look at your recommendations, I want to see quality over quantity. Ideally, recommendations should be from buyers of your service or products and not from colleagues touting your great personality and choice of restaurants. It is important for your recommendations to include specific reasons why someone enjoyed working with you.

- **Keep it updated.** If you aren't actively posting updates of value, which we will discuss later in this book, you are missing an opportunity to capture people's attention. By making frequent status updates, you can stay "top of mind" with potential prospects and buyers.

PRINCIPLE 4

The Algorithms Favor the Bold

MANTRA
i'll minimize my social platforms,
but i'll maximize their
latest features.

The world of social media is ever-changing. Even the savviest of marketers have a tough time keeping up. Earlier in the book, I encouraged you to forgo the temptation to jump on the newest social media site to become mainstream. Instead, stay the course and only plant your flag on a new platform if it makes sense for you or your business.

Once you've determined your top three platforms, I recommend using those platforms to their fullest extent—especially when they come out with a brand new feature. It has been our experience that social media sites prioritize content created within their latest features. For example, when Instagram first came out with Reels, many users noticed a big jump in views, likes, and comments. It was clear that Instagram wanted this feature to be adopted by the masses, so they gave an algorithm boost (showed our content to more people) when the new feature was used. Social media sites spend a lot of time and money on new feature adoption and want them to succeed. So, as a savvy content marketer, it would be wise to be early adopters and jump at the chance to experiment with their latest and greatest creations. Even if some new features don't make it as permanent additions, you'll reap the benefit of higher engagement for being both brave and bold!

What will the future be? I'm not sure—but the point is to always pay attention and keep up. When you focus only on a few social media platforms, it will leave you the bandwidth to stay on the cutting edge of those latest features.

KEY FEATURES YOU NEED TO TAKE ADVANTAGE OF:

- Newsletters
- Articles
- Carousel Posts

- Reels
- Stories
- Carousel Posts

As a speaker, capturing video has always been a top priority for me. My team would post those videos to social media and not be overly concerned with the length of each video. As the years went on and attention spans shrunk, social media platforms trended toward shorter videos. They also viewed vertical videos as a positive instead of a negative, like in years past. We saw the negative impact this was having on our views, likes, and other engagement metrics, so we went to work editing the original videos. We formatted the videos to make them vertical, brought the timing to under a minute, and even added music to some. We quickly saw a spike in all engagement metrics because we reformatted our videos into what the algorithms were looking for today. Will it trend back to longer timeframes in the future? I'm not sure … but we kept the originals just in case.

TAKE ACTION

1. Make sure your social media app is up to date.

2. Google 'New _____ features' and insert the social media site you're researching.

3. Evaluate the list and see if there are features you're not currently using.

4. Play with the platform. Every few months, I go to LinkedIn specifically looking for new features. Recently, I discovered I had the ability to use AI to assist me in creating content.

5. Subscribe to Hubspot's blog. They are a go-to resource for me to stay up to date on all things social media.

6. We are always experimenting with new features on my Instagram page—come check it out: instagram.com/CoreyPerlmanSpeaks

Never Forget That You're Easily Forgettable

MANTRA

i'll stay connected & in service to my audience until they're ready to buy from me.

When my friend first suggested life insurance to me, I was unmarried and had no kids. Every time he'd bring it up, my eyes would glaze over, and I'd pretend I was sleeping. Needless to say, I was not a prospect. A few years later, I had a child on the way and suddenly realized I needed some life insurance! The potential problem for my buddy was that I had moved away and since lost touch with him. Out of sight, out of mind. Fortunately for him, I check LinkedIn daily. During my daily scrolling, I just so happened to see a post from him about a charity golf outing he was attending. Right place, right time. He showed up when I was in 'buy mode' and, inevitably, got my business. He didn't have to send me postcards in the mail, or call me monthly to check in. Just staying connected on social media and consistently posting content was all it took.

There is an old sales adage that it takes seven touchpoints to convert a prospect into a customer. Arguably, that number has doubled and even tripled with the rise of digital media and the fall of attention spans.

We must fight the uphill battle of becoming forgotten by our prospects between the time they discover us and when they're ready to buy from us. That time can be days, months, or sometimes even years. By having a plan in place to connect with prospects on social media, we increase the chances of being remembered by them. And if, during that time, we can build trust and increase credibility with high-value content, then our chances to convert them to customers go up exponentially.

1. **CONNECT**

2. **COMMUNICATE**

3. **CONVERT!**

Below are some of my favorite ways to encourage prospects to follow or connect with you on social media.

1. **Contests.** People love to win stuff. As an example, we worked with a golf technology company whose followers got extremely motivated by the opportunity to win their cool products. Find the right contest or giveaway to motivate followers to connect!

2. **Ad Campaigns.** When you run a social media ad campaign, it's important to have a clear goal in place. When our clients are looking to increase their following, running a targeted ad for them to potential prospects is a quick and effective way to do so. We also run remarketing campaigns to target those who have visited our client's website in hopes that the visitor will follow them on social media.

3. **Cross-promotion.** Use your other marketing assets like blogs, podcasts, e-newsletters, or videos to encourage people to connect with you on your social platforms.

4. **Ask!** An easy and often overlooked strategy is to simply ask to connect with prospects. When we get a new lead, we often add them to our email database but forget to connect on LinkedIn. I would argue that a connection on LinkedIn is a better antidote for being forgotten than simply adding them to an email marketing list.

5. **Signage and QR Codes.** If you have a physical location, like a store or office, signage on display is a great way to encourage a social media connection. By using a QR Code, people can take out their phones and quickly get to your social media profiles. I recommend encouraging a connection with a special offer or discount.

Doing the above consistently will help you grow your social media audience. In future chapters, I'll share ways to avoid losing followers due to frustrating or annoying them.

All that matters is that they remember you—and I had to remind myself of this after hearing how this dentist began working with our agency. Four years after he heard me speak, the dentist called me to engage our marketing agency. When I asked him how he remembered me, he said he'd been following our business Facebook page. "That's funny. I never saw you like or comment on anything," I told him. He quickly responded, "Yeah, I don't really read them—I just see your name come up from time-to-time." Ouch! He went on to say that he knew the content was valuable—he just didn't have time to read the posts or watch the videos. In this case, it wasn't necessary that he gained value from my content but that he just had my name on his mind when he was ready to buy. It was a hit to my ego, but a sale nonetheless!

1. If LinkedIn is one of your top priorities, spend 30 minutes a week accepting connections and sending out connection requests.

2. If appropriate, create QR codes for your top social media sites so it's easy for people to find and follow you.

3. Try running a contest to create momentum and build followers quickly.

4. If Instagram or Facebook is a high priority, try creating an ad campaign with a specific goal to gain new followers.

5. Experiment by using trending or popular hashtags. Using hashtags can allow people to find your content who may not follow you.

SECTION TWO

Creating Compelling Content

2

The quality of your content will ultimately determine your success on social media. It's really that simple. When the content captivates, it gets people's attention and keeps them wanting to see more. In general, creating compelling content on a consistent basis is challenging—and when you're doing it for or on behalf of a business, it's exponentially more difficult. In other words, we have our work cut out for us. But it can be done—and this section will be your guide to getting there. Get ready to stop being boring, repetitive, and salesy and start being fun, interesting, and a valuable resource for your online audience.

Be Less Like the Squawking Parrot, More Like the Wise Owl

MANTRA
i will create consistent & compelling content.

I was chatting with a friend about how impressed I was with the content he'd been producing on LinkedIn. He smiled and told me he was simply trying to avoid being like the Squawking Parrot. That reference made me laugh, as I'd never heard it before. I asked him where he'd heard that, and he said, "From you, man! You said it in a presentation years ago when I was in your audience. I've never forgotten it and always try to avoid being that darn parrot when I'm posting to social media." It's funny how certain things we say stick with people. I don't recall ever using the analogy of the Squawking Parrot, but if it stuck with him, I hope it will stick with you!

A Squawking Parrot is loud, annoying, and painful on the ears. It will leave most people running for the nearest exit. This may be good for unwanted house guests but bad for your social media platforms.

Here are some common habits of the annoying Squawking Parrot and how to avoid becoming one:

- **They over promote.** Instead of organically finding ways to indirectly sell their value, their social media is filled with special offers, daily promotions, and other salesy content. When you oversell, you can easily frustrate and annoy people.

- **They cluster post.** Instead of spreading out their posts throughout the week, they post six or seven times in a matter of seconds. The cluster of posts end up littering your prospects' newsfeed. That's really annoying and is a quick way to get people to unfollow you!

- **They polarize their content.** By getting political with their posts, they will alienate at least half of their audience. Don't do it! Stay away from any topic that can turn your inlaw's Thanksgiving table into World War III and one that can cost you followers and customers.

- **They phone it in.** Just being on social media to check the boxes by posting syndicated articles, white papers, and other thoughtless documents isn't going to move the needle for their social media presence. Being on autopilot and having a platform that looks like a glorified brochure will be boring at worst, and stagnant at best.

- **They lack value.** Their posts are predominantly self-serving and offer very little relevant information to the audience. In a crowded and noisy environment, people lose interest and move on to other profiles that do a better job of delivering value.

Would your audience liken your social media content to the sounds of the Squawking Parrot?

Instead, be more like the Wise Owl. Listen to what your customers and clients want, and then address those desires by tailoring your social media strategy to them. Be thoughtful and intentional with an ultimate goal of adding value. Don't just talk about your products or services. Tell a digital story that includes many chapters that are all interesting and valuable to your audience.

Be a Wise Owl with the 5 Es:

- **Educate.** Wise owls take the time to teach people about topics related to the industry in which they have expertise. Giving away information and advice is a great way to gain respect and credibility from your audience.

- **Engage**. By being present and active on social platforms and making customers and prospects feel like you care, they will be more likely to interact with your content and likely be more inclined to do business with you. People like to feel a human connection, even through the internet.

- **Entertain.** They give the gift of laughter and bring light to an all-too-common negative place. They recognize the importance of making their social platform a place that people want to visit frequently and come to for the environment they provide.

- **Empower.** The Wise Owl provides the tools, resources, knowledge, and support needed to make a wise and educated buying decision. The content they provide is intended to serve the customer, not themselves.

- **Encourage.** Through testimonials, case studies, and other valuable information, they indirectly remind us that now is a great time to take action.

Let's keep these two beautiful birds atop our proverbial shoulders as a constant reminder to always strive to serve our audience instead of serving ourselves. Getting above the noise on social media can be difficult and challenging at times, but by being more like the Wise Owl than the Squawking Parrot, you will find more success with your social media platforms.

Recently, I spoke with one of our periodontal clients during one of our regular meetings, and he said something that really resonated with me. He told me that the more informed his prospective patients are before the consultation, the more likely they are to proceed with the service he recommended. He compared it to buying a car and the effort people put into researching that purchase before actually visiting the dealership. He said that when a patient has done their due diligence of his services and understands the benefits and risks and the differences between doctors and practices, the initial meeting is much more consultative and less salesy. He said, "The majority of the decision to proceed is made on their computer or phone before they even walk in the door."

He finished by saying, "And that's where you guys come in … when people visit our social media pages, they should have access to all the information they need and get all their questions answered. I want them to hear from other patients who have had the same types of services. I want them to virtually meet me and get a general sense of who I am while feeling confident that they are putting their teeth, gums, and smile into the right and capable hands."

With this feedback, we helped our client do just that. Now, when you visit his social platforms you will find:

- Video testimonials from previous patients.

- Terminology explanations by the doctor.

- Before and after pictures with video explanations from the doctor.

- A "Meet the Staff" section so prospective patients get to know the people who will see them upon their visit.

- Zoom interviews with other doctors on industry-specific topics.

Peruse your social media over the last three months. Are you:

1. Over-promoting?

2. Sharing content from others without adding your own perspective?

3. Only talking about yourself or your business?

4. Lacking consistency or a standard cadence?

5. Clogging up your audience's newsfeed by cluster-posting?

6. Telling people who to vote for?

If you answered yes to any of the above, you may be in danger of being the Squawking Parrot! Instead, be a Wise Owl by:

1. Focusing on adding value, rather than trying to sell.

2. Being present on your social media profiles by commenting and engaging with your audience.

3. Striving to serve your audience instead of serving yourself.

4. Encouraging your audience to take action by sharing testimonials, case studies, and other valuable information.

Talk in Terms of Their Interest, Not Your Own

MANTRA

i'll create content with my audience at the forefront of my mind.

This is an abbreviated version of Dale Carnegie's famous principle, and it's just as relevant today as ever before. Make it about your audience. It's that simple. It's the platinum rule of social media and the guiding principle behind many of the chapters that follow. We've all seen the pages cluttered with articles and promotional material, and we run from them. They are too salesy and are not the intended purpose of social media. Social media is a two-way conversation, and the most successful brands focus on providing value and building relationships with their audience.

Here are some questions that should always come before posting to social media:

1. Is this serving my audience or self-serving?

2. How am I adding value with this post?

3. What question am I answering? What problem am I solving?

4. Will people benefit from what I'm about to share?

The answer doesn't always have to be "yes" to any of the questions above, but should be considered before every post. If you're answering "no" more often than not, it might be time to reconsider your content strategy.

Every time I connect with someone on LinkedIn, and they immediately send me their sales pitch, a car salesman angel gets his gold-plated cufflinks. It happens daily. Does this strategy ever actually work? Have you successfully removed the terrible taste in your mouth of someone connecting with you just to sell you something and then acted on their spammy pitch? Well, you'd be the first. It's a yucky strategy that adds fuel to the anti-social media fire. Let's be part of the solution, not the problem.

Connect with people who you can support and who can support you. Then, stay laser-focused on delivering value. It's that simple. If you stop reading this book right now, that in and of itself will foster higher engagement. Just be helpful, entertaining, funny, or provocative. Any of those can reside under the value category. If they value you, they'll never leave. And when they're ready to buy, you'll be there.

 My friend Bill is a local real estate agent and has worked hard to build his local social media following. Although he had a significant amount of connections and followers, his engagement (likes, comments, shares, clicks) was non-existent. When I scrolled through his posts, they all looked the same—house, house, house, house. I challenged Bill to mix in content that had nothing to do with real estate but was still valuable to his audience. A week later, as I navigated my newsfeed, a post came up from Bill. It was a map and subsequent link to all the best local Christmas holiday light displays. Bingo. It was timely, as kids were out on holiday break, and tremendously valuable to us parents desperately looking for ways to entertain our kids. He had more engagement on that single post than any other post the previous two weeks combined.

Bill realized that to truly add value to his audience, he had to be more than just a local real estate directory. They could get that anywhere. He wanted to be the source for a unique mix of local content that anyone new or familiar to Roswell, Georgia, would find interesting. His content was authentic, relevant, valuable, and completely on brand, as it was all about the city he loves and where he helps people buy and sell homes.

TAKE ACTION

Here are some ways to ensure you're adding value to your audience:

1. Answer frequently asked questions from customers and prospects.

2. Post practical tips and advice that can help your audience solve problems or achieve their goals.

3. Curate content that is already getting good engagement. You can sift through the noise and only share content worthy of your followers' time.

4. Share content that entertains and delights your audience, such as memes, jokes, or behind-the-scenes glimpses of your brand.

5. Ask for feedback and suggestions from your audience on what types of content they would like to see from your brand. This can help you tailor your posts to your audience's needs and interests, ensuring you're adding value in a way that resonates.

Talk More about Your Baristas, Less about Your Coffee

MANTRA

i will humanize my brand by highlighting my people.

I'm a habitual Starbucks visitor. And not just any Starbucks, but a particular Starbucks just a few miles from my house. Friends of mine would jokingly refer to it as "Corey's Starbucks," as they'd see me there, in my same chair, day in and day out. I enjoyed other local coffee shops for their specialty coffee but still found myself at "Corey's Starbucks" more often than not. The reason why? The people! The Starbucks baristas took the time to get to know me, and I found myself looking forward to my almost daily work sessions. Their investment in getting to know me and the drinks I preferred created my unwavering loyalty to that location.

My intention here is not to shamelessly plug Starbucks (I have just as much love for the local coffee shops in our area) but instead to remind us how important people are to the success of a brand or business. So why wouldn't we highlight them on social media? Why not show the world just how amazing our team is and why working with them is the best decision a prospect could ever make?

People want to feel connected to the company or individual they interact with and not just simply be a patron. They want to know about the culture, values, and other shared interests of the people and brands they support. When you pull back the proverbial curtain and show the people behind your brand, you increase trust, credibility, and overall buyer confidence.

Here are a few additional benefits to highlighting employees on social media:

1. **Boost Employee Morale.** When you feature your employees on social media, it gives them a sense of recognition and validation for their hard work and contributions.

2. **Build a Positive Company Culture.** Showcasing employees' achievements and milestones helps demonstrate what the company prioritizes.

3. **Employee Advocacy.** When you highlight employees on social media, they are more likely to share and engage with the content.

4. **Recruitment and Talent Acquisition.** Positive employee experiences shared on social media can enhance the company's

perception and can help attract top talent when recruiting new employees.

5. **Social Responsibility and Diversity.** Highlighting employees with diverse backgrounds and showcasing the company's social responsibility initiatives can show commitment to sustainability, inclusivity, and community engagement.

Jessica and Christine own a mortgage company and came to our agency with concerns over low engagement on their social media. No matter what was tried, they couldn't get above a few likes or comments on any given post. The owners, Jessica and Christine, shared they had a fun and vibrant team of loan officers and, as a team, spent a lot of time giving back to their community. We decided to cut back on talking solely about interest rates and housing news. Instead, we asked Jessica and Christine to give their audience a glimpse into the people behind the brand. The new strategy included sharing pictures and videos of the team and highlighting their hobbies, interests, and passions. Our team would use Instagram Stories and Reels to highlight their involvement in community events. Because team members were tagged in these posts, they were happy to share and engage with the content. Soon, friends, colleagues, and the community began to interact, and all engagement numbers trended upward.

Jessica and Christine now love their social media channels because it gives people a peek into the fun and vibrant culture they've created. Beyond better engagement metrics, they also shared with us that it has helped with employee recruitment. Potential employees want to know if they align with a company's culture, and social media can be a great starting point for them.

TAKE ACTION

Make a target list of team members you can highlight on your social media. Ask them to do brief selfie videos answering a few questions. If they're camera shy, they can write out their answers, and you can post to social media with a fun, authentic photo of their choosing. I've offered some questions below you can use to get started:

1. What inspired you to join our company, and what do you enjoy most about working here?

2. What are some of your biggest accomplishments or contributions to the company?

3. What advice would you give someone interested in pursuing a career in your field?

4. What are some of your hobbies or interests outside of work?

5. What's a fun fact about yourself that most people at work don't know?

6. What are some of the things you appreciate about the company culture, and how do they align with your personal values?

Don't Tell Me, Show Me

MANTRA
Video will be a fundamental
piece of my overall digital
strategy.

No matter the platform, social media sites consistently favor video more than all other forms of content. Beyond the benefit of the algorithm boost you will trigger, using video will help your passion, enthusiasm, and charisma shine through more effectively to your audience. Video does not need to eliminate or replace articles and other forms of written content, but it is often a good alternative or strong addition to incorporate into your regular social media strategy.

What kind of content lends itself to a good video? Here are 3 examples of times to use a video post:

1. **If it's TL;DR (Too Long, Didn't Read).** In the digital age, people either don't have time or don't want to take the time to read paragraphs on social media. If you have a lot to say, I suggest saying it on video. Two paragraphs of text can be said in under a minute, and people will be more willing to absorb the information you share.

2. **When you have something you want your viewer to visualize.** It's always more exciting to **see** a house, new smile, vacation spot, etc. than to read about it.

3. **When you have something to say.** If you're going to teach, educate, or otherwise add value—say it on camera. Many times, we retain information more easily when we watch and listen rather than read. In most cases, you can do both, so shoot the video and add captions so people can read along!

If you've used video content to post before, you already know that there are many different ways you can share it. You can stream live or upload pre-recorded video content. You can also chop up the video into a Reel or Story on Instagram and post it to other locations like your YouTube or Vimeo channel. If you plan to shoot live video, just remember that … well … it's live! So treat it like a news broadcast and be ready to roll with the punches. With pre-recorded video, you can take time to edit both during and after you shoot, so the finished product is more polished and refined.

Here are a few other ways our clients have used video on their social media:

- On location (at an event, showroom, destination, etc.).

- Virtual tour (real estate, hotel, office, vehicle).

- Video series (Ask the Expert, Motivation Monday, Fun Fridays).

- Promotional video (launch of a new product, commercial, testimonial montage).

Using video for a virtual tour, a behind-the-scenes look, or an impassioned message sharing your values will always translate with the audience more effectively and more personally. It's also good to note that video can still be used and translated into written copy, like a newsletter or blog post.

Additional Video Tips:

- **Spend time on the title.** A compelling title must hook the viewer to stop what they're doing and watch your video. You should spend as much time on the title as you do the content of the video. It's that important.

- **Don't bury the lead.** You sell someone on the rest of your video within the first ten seconds. Make those seconds count. Tell us exactly what you plan to cover, and make sure what you say really grabs your audience's attention.

- **Use captions.** According to Digiday.com, 75% of people watch videos without the sound turned on. Don't let your viewers miss your content because they don't know what you are saying.

- **Capture it, don't create it.** Don't overthink your video. Focus on capturing everyday moments and using those in your content. Take a look at your camera roll. I bet your next post is already there!

Lastly, always keep the 3 C's in mind when shooting video:

1. **C**learly state your point.

2. **C**onfidently share your message.

3. Keep it **C**oncise!

Our dear friend Cindy owned a beautiful and quaint bed and breakfast called The Purple Martin Inn. She came to me looking for guidance on how to use social media to make her charming secret paradise not so secret anymore. As I scanned her profiles and business pages, I saw beautiful pictures of the Inn and the lovely surroundings in the charming town of Rogers City, Michigan. Considering the pages were lacking engagement and activity, I knew from experience that something must be missing, but it wasn't glaringly obvious at first.

Cindy invited my family and me to stay at the Inn over the summer. We fell in love with the place, and even more so, Cindy! My family experienced the abundance of passion and enthusiasm she radiated as she showed us around, and even my young children were captivated by our entertaining tour guide. As we walked, it suddenly became apparent why Cindy's place was called The Purple Martin Inn. She had created a sanctuary for Purple Martins, a beautiful bird native to Brazil that travels to Michigan for the summer months. At Cindy's sanctuary, these birds lived their best lives and were treated like her children. It was a beautiful scene where she knew precisely how many came each year and how many babies were in each nest. It was sweet to watch her revel in the magical place she created.

During our visit, I sat down with Cindy to share my observations with her. The magic of The Purple Martin Inn was not coming through on social media. The Purple Martin Inn's digital identity needed more Cindy and, specifically, her beautiful relationship with these birds. We came up with a game plan that included videos of Cindy's famous tours, as well as live updates of her precious purple martins. She immediately gained a huge bump in engagement, and Cindy had multiple inquiries on her Facebook page about staying at her inn. She became a go-to resource for purple martins, and bird lovers everywhere were excited to visit The Purple Martin Inn.

Being Authentically Social is about offering a unique and personalized experience and doubling down on what differentiates you from others. Cindy was a special lady, and it was evident by the way she radiated on camera. Because her birds offered a unique experience unlike any other, they should be the primary focus of the inn's marketing strategy. The inn's page engagement soared when the purple martins became the heroes of the social media posts.

In loving memory of Cindy Vezinau. We love you, Cindy, and will forever remember you and all the fond memories at The Purple Martin Inn.

TAKE ACTION

I invite you to take my *one-take challenge:*

1. Decide on the content of your video. What is your message? What do you want to share with your audience?

2. Choose the platform(s) where you'll share your video.

3. Find a good location to shoot your video. I always suggest being 'in the wild' or on location (e.g., at the job site for a home remodeler) as it makes for a much more interesting video.

4. Use the 3 Cs: Clear, Confident, and Concise!

5. If you make a mistake, just keep going! This is the one-take challenge!

6. Once complete, add a catchy title.*

7. When you create a video post, add content that entices people to want to watch.

8. Add captions so people can read along while you talk.

9. Add appropriate hashtags.

10. Post it!

Bonus: Picking a catchy title is critical. Titles that drive the most engagement are ones that are easy to grasp and tell you exactly what you are about to watch. Titles using phrases like *"Three things to avoid"* or *"Five ways to increase"* are typically most attractive to viewers and are the most likely to get your video watched.

Make Your Customers the Hero in Your Digital Story

MANTRA
i will make it less about me, more about them.

Since my family recently finished the Harry Potter movie series (all eight of them!), I'd like to share an analogy for the role our customers should play in our digital story. Our clients should be the hero, Harry, while the business owner should be the guide, Dumbledore, who helps Harry along his heroic journey. Dumbledore was always quick to remind the world that Harry was special and that he was the reason that good would ultimately prevail. Dumbledore loved nothing more than watching Harry get the credit he deserved. By highlighting our customers on social media, we indirectly promote our products or services to others who might be interested in doing business with us. It seems less self-serving but still demonstrates our value to the audience. When Dumbledore got in trouble, it was Harry who told the world the truth about his friend. When our customers take to social media to share their experiences, it comes off as more trustworthy and credible than if we said it ourselves.

Here are some ways to focus your social media content on your customers:

1. **Share customer success stories and testimonials.** Share stories of how your products or services have helped your customers achieve their goals, solve problems, or improve their lives. Testimonials from satisfied customers can also be powerful social proof that will influence potential customers.

2. **Highlight customer-created content.** Share photos, videos, or other content created by your customers that feature your products or services. This not only shows your appreciation for their support, but can also encourage other customers to create and share their own content.

3. **Feature customer interviews.** Conduct interviews with your customers and share them on social media. This can be a great way to showcase their experiences with your brand and provide insights into how they use your products or services.

4. **Collaborate with customers.** Partner with your customers on social media to create content or initiatives that benefit both your brand and their personal or professional goals. This can be a great way to build strong relationships and create mutually beneficial outcomes.

Overall, showcasing customers on social media is an effective way to build stronger relationships, establish trust, and grow your brand. By highlighting your customers, you can create a community of loyal supporters who feel connected to your brand and are more likely to engage with your content and, ultimately, your services.

One of my dear friends, Ross Bernstein, is one of the busiest professional speakers on the planet. When I ask him about his success, he always jokes that it's not due to social media—because he believes he really doesn't know how to do it or what he is doing. The truth is, Ross does a perfect job of shining the spotlight on his clients. Each time Ross leaves the stage, he immediately goes to LinkedIn and thanks the client for giving him the opportunity to speak. He shares wonderful attributes about the company or association and keeps the attention fully on them. He tags all the people associated with the event (the Harry Potters) and ends the post thanking them for their hospitality and kindness. These posts perform extremely well for Ross on social media and are a gentle reminder to other event planners hoping for a similar experience. I often share Ross's strategy as a best practice for truly making it about others instead of ourselves. Ross continues to believe he knows nothing about social media, but I hope a best practice in a social media book will finally convince him otherwise.

TAKE ACTION

Evaluate your digital marketing content.

1. Who's the hero in your posts? Is it mostly you?

2. How often do you post about your customers?

3. Write down three customers that would be good candidates for an interview, case study, or testimonial.

Get creative about the ways you can make customers the heroes of your social media strategy.

When in Doubt, Go Local

MANTRA
i will make being local my competitive advantage.

I recently spoke to an association of credit unions, and I asked them what they believe differentiates them from the bigger banks. One person answered, "We are rooted in the community—our customers are our neighbors."

"I love that answer," I quickly responded. "If you're a local business, your social media should be synonymous with the culture, values, and history of your great community." By highlighting local events, attractions, and other small businesses on social media, you'll become a valued resource for your audience while also supporting your local community.

Here are some different ways to support and highlight your local community:

1. **Feature local events and activities.** Share photos and updates from local events and activities, such as festivals, farmers markets, or charity events. This can help promote your community and demonstrate your involvement and support.

2. **Highlight local landmarks and attractions.** Share photos and information about local landmarks and attractions, such as parks, museums, or historical sites. This can help showcase the unique character and charm of your community.

3. **Collaborate with local businesses.** Partner with other local businesses to cross-promote each other's products and services on social media. This can help build stronger relationships with other businesses in your community and attract new customers.

4. **Support local causes and charities.** Share information about local causes and charities that your business supports, and encourage your followers to get involved as well. This can help position your business as a socially responsible member of the community.

5. **Use local hashtags.** Use hashtags specific to your local community in your social media posts. This can help increase your visibility within the community and connect with potential customers searching for local businesses.

My friend Eric owns apartment buildings in the trendy town of Royal Oak, Michigan. He was looking for ways to attract and engage a younger audience to take tours of his modernized apartments. Eric took to social media with a laser focus on the Royal Oak community. Rarely did he talk about his apartments. Instead, his brand's social media became a resource for new members of that community. You'd find reviews of restaurants, fun things to do, and local collaborations. If online visitors needed information on his apartment community, it was always quick and easy to find. But the primary focus was on the community and all that it had to offer. Eric was blown away by the results. Since starting this marketing strategy, his occupancy rate never dipped below 90%. He attributed much of that success to the hyper-local focus of his social media profiles.

TAKE ACTION

1. Designate Saturday as *Small Biz Saturday* and highlight a local business in your area.

   a. If you visit the business, tag them in a social media post and include a photo or video.

   b. You can also create a post during the week and schedule it to go out on Saturday if you want to keep your weekends free from social media.

   c. Don't forget to use local hashtags (#smallbizsaturday).

   d. Participate in the official Small Business Saturday which happens every year in November.

2. If your community hosts seasonal events, add them to your content calendar and promote them on your social media pages.

3. Think of a business (or group of businesses) you can collaborate with, and consider a social media partnership. You can cross-promote on each other's social media profiles and even host events together.

Doing Good Is Good for Business

MANTRA
i know that people want to do business with people doing good work in the world.

During an episode of Andy Stanley's Leadership Podcast, I heard his guest, Jeff Henderson, talk about the *community* as one of the groups every organization should be for. And then he said a line that hit me like a ton of bricks. He said, "Doing good is good for business". That line really resonated with me, as it has proven to be true for both me and my clients. More than ever before, people want to know what a business stands for and the impact it has on the community and world. A company's core values and mission can be a key determining factor in a person's overall buying decision. Social media provides a perfect place to share the good we are doing in the world and help connect us to our customers on a deeper level.

Here are some examples of ways businesses are doing good in the world. Any of these would be worthy of being part of your overall digital story.

1. **Support Nonprofits and Charities.** Partner with reputable nonprofits or charitable organizations and share updates about the positive impact of these partnerships. Use social media to raise awareness about their causes.

2. **Corporate Social Responsibility (CSR) Initiatives.** Engage in various CSR programs, such as supporting local communities, environmental conservation, education, or promoting social causes. Share updates, photos, and success stories from these initiatives on social media platforms.

3. **Transparent and Ethical Practices.** Showcase your commitment to ethical business practices, fair labor conditions, and sustainable sourcing. Share behind-the-scenes content that highlights how your business operates responsibly.

4. **Employee Well-Being.** Demonstrate your concern for employee well-being by promoting work-life balance, professional development programs, and inclusive workplace practices. Share employee testimonials and success stories.

5. **Crisis Response and Support.** During times of crisis or natural disasters, use your social media platforms to inform and support those affected. Show empathy and sensitivity in your messaging.

6. **Positive Storytelling.** Use storytelling techniques to share inspiring stories of individuals or communities that have benefited from your business's initiatives. This humanizes your brand and helps build a positive image.

At our agency, Impact Social Media, one of our core values is IMPACT. We make it a priority to collaborate with our clients on ways to make an impact in their community. Every year, we ask our clients to nominate a local charity that needs some digital marketing direction and a social media makeover. Our team picks out a few non-profit organizations, and we facilitate a free private consulting session. We spend a few hours with these wonderful organizations to refresh their brand and fine-tune their online marketing strategy. I can speak for my entire team when I say it's the highlight of our year. It feels so good to give back in a meaningful way that has a direct impact on their organization. Together with our clients, we share these impactful stories on social media, and it's a hit with both of our audiences.

TAKE ACTION

1. How are you giving back to your community?

2. What organizations or non-profits does your business support?

3. How does your business demonstrate commitment to diversity and inclusion?

4. What steps does the business take to minimize its environmental footprint?

5. Is there anything else you or your business is doing that is bringing good to the world?

Make sure your answers are part of your digital story. People love good news and are happy to share it with others. Here is an opportunity to spread light in what's often a dark and negative platform.

Let Your Customers Do the Talking

MANTRA
i will never let a verbal
testimonial go unpublished.

I had just finished a presentation for the performance racing industry, and a gentleman came up to the front of the room to ask a question. During our conversation, he said some really kind things about my talk and the value it would bring to his business. As he started to walk away, he turned around and said, "You didn't follow your own advice!" I knew right away what he meant. I had just told the audience to never let a verbal testimonial go unpublished. I smiled, waved him back over, and pulled out my phone. I hit record, and he restated the kind words he shared just a few moments ago. Within minutes, that testimonial video was on my LinkedIn profile. Before he left, we took a photo together on his camera, and he committed to posting his feedback on his profiles as well.

We spend so much of our time focusing on creating and putting out our very best content that we often miss the golden opportunities to allow our customers to do the talking. As discussed in principle #9, we should make efforts to highlight our clients and customers. We should also put that same amount of focus into thinking about ways we can get our clients and customers to actually post about us.

Think about a time when you were going to make a purchase that was important to you. Did you check the reviews? What did those reviews do for your confidence in that product or service? Positive reviews are critical and should be a priority for your overall digital footprint. The weight these reviews carry should never be underestimated. Focus on creating a great experience for your customers, and then encourage them to post about their experience online.

Here are some places to request positive feedback from your customers:

1. **Direct Posts and Videos.** Social platforms such as Facebook, Instagram, Twitter (X), and TikTok. Make sure they properly tag your business so you are sure to not miss the kind words.

2. **LinkedIn Recommendation.** Your LinkedIn profile is the perfect place to let your customers share their positive experience about working with you or your business.

3. **Post Reviews.** Review sites such as Yelp, TripAdvisor, and Google My Business are great platforms for customers to share their experiences with others.

I find that people are often more motivated to leave reviews when they're upset or unhappy about a product or service. None of us are perfect, and occasionally, customers may be unhappy with some part of their experience. If that is the case, it should be our job to try to fix that problem. Often, by listening and taking in the customer feedback, we can correct the issue and turn the experience around for the customer or client, which will give them the opportunity to shift their perception of the experience. Acknowledge, apologize, and amend the problem the best you can. Then, don't be afraid to ask if they'd consider editing or reposting their previous review.

When you're doing good work—and your customers and clients have voiced their appreciation—don't assume they will share their experience online. While you may be confident in their good intentions, people are busy and posting about their good experiences is often not a top priority. Find ways to make this quick and convenient by having a process in place that works well for both you and your customers. Give them easy access to your review pages (like a QR Code), increasing your chances of getting their review. If the situation calls for it, ask them to tag you in a post where they can share their happy experience with others.

If you are struggling to be so direct in asking for reviews at first, you may feel more comfortable doing so by giving an incentive in an email. Let them know you recognize they are happy with your service, and ask if they'd mind posting a review. Assure them that you recognize that this takes time out of their day and that you know their time is valuable. For example, many of our clients offer $5 co-branded Starbucks cards as a thank-you-a-latte for doing business and considering writing a review. Because they're giving them the gift card, regardless of whether the review is completed or not, it feels less like a bribe and more of a token of appreciation. Even if you don't get the review, the gesture will be remembered and appreciated.

My family recently took a trip of a lifetime on a cruise through Alaska. We had an amazing travel advisor, Judy, who took care of us from start to finish. She worked with us to ensure we had everything we needed to feel completely safe and comfortable and even sent us a welcome packet days before we set sail. Inside that welcome packet was also a handwritten note from her. The note read, "I hope you have an amazing adventure, and if you're having the time of your life and you feel so inclined, please take a moment to share your experience on social media. Tag me so I can watch and enjoy your adventure as well. It would mean the world to me." You see, Judy knew that the chance of us posting to social media was most likely to happen on or right after the trip, and she knew exactly when to ask for positive feedback. Three days into our trip, we were sitting on the ship, enjoying the sunshine and a pina colada, and I took out my phone to capture the moment. I remembered Judy's request and shared a heartfelt message about our trip and how she made it all happen. I shared the post on my social media and made sure to tag Judy. Job well done, Judy. Job well done!

Create a process for getting positive reviews.

1. Do you or your business have an active process to get 4 and 5-star reviews?

2. When's the right time to ask for a review from a happy customer?

3. How can you make the process of giving the positive reviews efficient and easy for the customer?

4. Would it make sense to ask for LinkedIn recommendations? Request a recommendation on their LinkedIn profile and customize the message to let them know what you'd like them to say. This makes the process easy and efficient for the person leaving you a recommendation.

5. Do you have any Facebook reviews? If not, consider how you can get them.

6. Do your customers engage in Instagram comments? How can you get them to speak highly of you there?

As I mentioned earlier, we typically need to motivate people to write positive reviews. When we have a process in place, it is much easier to get them to do so. As an example, my process for getting LinkedIn recommendations goes like this: Two days after one of my speaking events, I will send an email to the meeting planner who hired me and request a LinkedIn recommendation. I let them know I was happy to get the opportunity to speak and ask for their feedback. Then, I will finish by asking for their LinkedIn recommendation. If I wait a week or two to send the email, chances are they may not even respond.

More Funny, More Money

MANTRA
i will be the light & give the
gift of laughter.

The world is not a perfect place, and if we need proof of this, we can usually turn to social media. Social media has a negative connotation because of how negative it has become. But where there's a challenge, there's an opportunity! How can we create or share more content that brings a smile, giggle, or even a belly laugh to our audience? The ability to keep things light and offer levity is often a great way to gain engagement from your audience.

Here are a few ways to use humor in your digital story:

1. **Use memes.** Memes are a popular way to inject humor into social media content. Use memes relevant to your brand or industry to create funny and relatable content. Remember, some memes are copyrighted, so use your best judgment here.

2. **Make puns.** Play with words and use puns to create funny captions or titles for your social media posts.

3. **Create humorous videos.** Create short, funny videos that showcase your brand's personality and sense of humor. These videos can be used to highlight your products or services in a humorous way.

4. **Use emojis.** Emojis are a great way to add humor to your social media posts. Use them to create funny captions or to replace words in your posts.

5. **Share funny quotes.** Share funny quotes or jokes relevant to your industry or brand. This can help create a sense of community and build engagement with your audience.

6. **Show behind-the-scenes bloopers.** Share behind-the-scenes bloopers or outtakes of your videos or photo shoots. This can help showcase the human side of your brand and show your authenticity.

7. **Use humor to address common problems.** Use humor to address common problems or complaints that your customers might have. This can help defuse tension and show that your brand is approachable and willing to address issues in a humorous way.

Humor can be overdone, so try not to be excessive. This is your business, and, for the most part, people expect value and education. Find ways to pepper humor in and play with the frequency. We often suggest dedicating Fridays for humor. You can call it Fun Friday and dedicate that day to laughter.

We have a flooring client, and the owner, Jason, is a really funny guy. We decided to use that to our advantage. We video Jason out on location to share details about the flooring jobs, but we make sure he does it in his own unique way. Each video has some off-the-cuff content that wasn't scripted and makes the video fun to watch. We intentionally keep Jason's personality front and center in all the videos we shoot because people really resonate with his spontaneity and humor. It works for his brand. So, if you're funny, charismatic, or witty, give yourself permission to let that out when you're shooting a video. Your personality will shine through, and people will love to watch and engage.

1. **Define Your Brand's Humor Style.** Before you start adding humor to your social media, it's important to define your brand's humor style. Are you going for slapstick comedy, witty humor, or sarcastic jokes? Understanding your brand's humor style will help you create content that is consistent with your brand's voice and message.

2. **Know Your Audience.** Understanding your audience is key to adding humor to your social media. Know what types of humor your audience enjoys, and tailor your content to their preferences. This will help ensure your humor is well-received and engages your audience.

3. **Use Real-Life Scenarios.** Using real-life scenarios is a great way to add humor to your social media. Share funny stories or situations that have happened to you or your team. This can help showcase the human side of your brand and help you be more authentic.

4. **Keep it Appropriate.** While humor is a great way to connect with your audience, it's important to keep it culturally appropriate. Avoid controversial topics or humor that could be offensive to certain groups of people. You don't want to risk alienating your audience or damaging your brand's reputation. #DontBeAJerk

5. **Use Visuals.** Visuals such as images or videos can help enhance the humor in your social media content. Use images or videos relevant to your humor style and message. This can help make your content even more engaging and shareable.

6. **Test and Measure.** Test different types of humor and measure the engagement and response from your audience. This can help you understand what types of humor work best for your brand and audience, while refining your approach over time.

7. **Be Consistent.** Consistency is key when it comes to adding humor to your social media. Make sure your humor style is consistent across all your social media channels and that your humor is in line with your brand's values and message.

SECTION THREE

Efficiency

Creating compelling content consistently is a full-time job. In fact, it can be multiple full-time jobs. It's not easy, and that's why so many choose to automate and produce lackluster content. Efficiency is the key to keeping your sanity. Whether you're in charge of your social media or others run it for you, this section will help you maximize resources and minimize redundancies.

3

Keep Your Sanity with a Content Calendar

MANTRA
i will have a plan & avoid the dreaded, 'What should we post today?'

When our team onboards a new client, we always establish multiple categories (or buckets) of content. We pick four or five categories that make the most sense for their business and dedicate a day of the week to each of those categories. Every piece of content we create for their social platforms can fit into one of these buckets. Creating these buckets in collaboration with the client helps for the following reasons:

1. It requires both our client and us to **be on the same page** with the overall content strategy.

2. We can **ensure that each bucket has enough content.** For example, if one of the buckets is testimonials and it is empty, we can quickly reach out to the client to help refill the bucket.

3. It makes it **easy to keep the client involved.** If they know Friday's bucket is local good news, and they come across a feel-good story, they know it is content we'd love them to send over.

4. It is truly a **collaborative experience.** If the client knows Thursday is *Thank You Thursday,* they're always looking for opportunities to give shout-outs or thank yous on their social media. They pass along those ideas, and our team can take care of the implementation.

5. It is **visual**. Together, we can quickly look at the buckets and see if there is anything we're missing. We also prioritize the buckets and add percentages. For example, the promotion bucket is often priority #1 and might get 25% of the overall content.

I'm a huge fan of **creating Buckets of Content for your digital marketing strategy**. Each bucket gets filled with content that eventually gets deployed on social media in the coming weeks. We always leave room for flexibility if something comes up that takes priority or we decide it is not a good idea to post that day. The calendar is never set in stone but is a great guide for all businesses.

I'm often asked if our buckets change depending on the social platform. The way we publish the content changes depending on the social platform we're posting on, but the buckets rarely change. For example, the same testimonial will look much different on Facebook than on Instagram. Facebook may have a link in the description, while Instagram may have 7–10 hashtags instead.

Here's an example of what a typical client content calendar might look like for a given week:

1. **Monday is Motivation Monday.** Content that can inspire or empower to get the week started.

2. **Tuesday is Testimonial Tuesday.** Tuesday is dedicated to showcasing customers and letting them do the talking about your business.

3. **WTF Wednesday.** This does not mean what you think it means! It means What To Film Wednesday and is dedicated to shooting a video and getting it posted to social media.

4. **Thursday is Thank You Thursday.** Thank a client, community member, or business. This is your opportunity to shine the spotlight on others.

5. **Fun Fact Friday or Fun Friday.** This is an opportunity to share an obscure fact about your industry, or just a funny and relatable post to get the weekend started.

6. **Small Business Saturday.** As mentioned in principle #11, Saturday can be reserved for highlighting a favorite local business in your area.

Note: I'm often asked about posting content on the weekends. This very much depends on the industry, as some audiences frequent social media on the weekends while others don't. My suggestion is to research if your audience is active on social media during the weekend, and if so, schedule some posts to be delivered on those days.

Content is the most important—yet most difficult—part of social media marketing. Having a content calendar with dedicated categories will make life easier for the business and those managing your social media.

Our team works with a family physician's association, and they have multiple events going on at the same time throughout the year. Besides events, they educate on advocacy and policy, spotlight physician members, and so much more. It wasn't a surprise to find their social media profiles to be a hodgepodge of posts with no consistency or cohesiveness. Together, we created six categories of content scheduled for a specific day of the week that made the most sense. Here's what we came up with for them:

CONTENT CALENDAR	MONDAY	TUESDAY	WEDNESDAY
	· Local Chapter Meeting · Webinar Promo	· Partners In Health · Case Studies	· Show & Tell · Homeroom Continuing Education
	#MondayMotivation	#TestimonialTuesday	#WednesdayWisdom
	THURSDAY	**FRIDAY**	**ROTATING**
	· Event Promotion · Latest Blog Post	· Featured Family Physician · Workshops	· Reels/Animated Posts · FM Docs Store · National Days · Partner Resources
	#ThursdayThoughts	#FeatureFriday	

We meet monthly as a team and ensure we have enough content for each category. This has resulted in being able to tell their full digital story, not just one aspect of the association. Our client appreciates the accountability it creates, and they know exactly what we need from them at any given time. It's truly a win-win!

1. What are the 5–6 categories of content that make the most sense for your business?

2. Which days of the week will you post to each platform? Assign a category to an appropriate day of the week.

3. Create a recurring monthly meeting to review content for the previous and upcoming month. Does each category (bucket) have adequate content? Ensure you are also using the appropriate features for your content (Reels, Stories, etc.) to receive maximum engagement.

A content calendar helps you create a plan to post the right content to the right digital platform at the right time.

Be Active on Social Media Without Being on Social Media

MANTRA
My mental health is
my priority.

I have a secret I've been avoiding telling you until now.

I don't post to my social media accounts. I have given way to the experts for a few reasons. First, I don't like the way it makes me feel more often than not. Second, it is a full-time job to keep up with all the feature updates and design trends needed to create engaging, compelling content. I spend around 15 minutes a day and often take weeks off of Instagram and Facebook. And yet, my profiles are updated almost every day. How is it possible to achieve this and still be authentic? Because I always create the content.

I do all my content creation offline. This includes articles, videos, and any content you see on my profiles. My social media team then takes that content and formats it to fit the intended platform. This might include copyediting, graphic design, video editing, and anything else needed to make it the right size, shape and format for social media. My responsibilities do not require me to be on social media, and that's a gift I've been able to give myself. I trust my team's capabilities to take it from written or video form and turn it into snack-able content for social media. I will give them the written copy that goes with the post, offer hashtag suggestions, and people to tag. They execute. It's truly a match made in heaven.

Here are just some ways my team transforms my content into engaging social media content:

1. **Images.** They find and include eye-catching visuals to capture the attention of my audience and make my content more memorable.

2. **Formats.** They may use different image sizes, video lengths, or caption lengths for different platforms.

3. **Captions.** Add accurate captions to videos so people can watch your videos with the sound off.

4. **Flare.** Add music and animations.

5. **Tag You're It.** Include relevant hashtags to increase visibility and reach a wider audience.

6. **Branding.** Create borders or frames around images to make them more eye-catching and consistent with my branding.

There's a lot that goes into creating quality social media content, and I knew I wasn't the right person for the job.

So, where do I spend my limited time on social media? I engage with other people's content and respond to comments on my posts. I will dive deeper into this strategy in an upcoming chapter.

I recently attended a speaking industry conference called Influence. It was so great to see old friends and fellow speakers I hadn't connected with in years. I snapped some selfies and, without thinking, posted them to my Instagram feed. A few minutes later, they had disappeared. That's right, my team had deleted them. What?!? Why?!? I later found out that I had messed up my overall Instagram grid - something they had spent quite some time getting just right. They were already collecting photos from my conference experience and planned to put them in a story that would garner more engagement and look better as a collection. They had a plan, and I was stepping on their proverbial toes. I love that they take pride in my profile, and I was perfectly fine with being overruled. Like I said earlier, they are the experts!

1. What's your current relationship with social media? Are you okay with the time you're spending, or are you also looking for ways to disconnect?

2. Do you have the time needed to get the job done right?

3. Do you have the expertise?

4. Are there others around you that could do it better? A staff member, intern, family member, or outside agency?

5. Block time in your calendar to create content. This time can be spent writing articles, shooting videos, or brainstorming topic ideas for social media. Once you have your social media resource in place, you can create a process for sending over your content and letting the expert do the social media posting.

Make AI Your Personal Assistant

MANTRA
i will not fear the future;
i'll embrace it!

When ChatGPT (a common Artificial Intelligence software) started to become mainstream, I got a flood of emails asking how concerned I was for the future of our social media agency. Will this kill your business? Will you fire your employees and just hire robots? Those were real questions I received, and I'm sure I wasn't alone in addressing these concerns. Luckily, I've had lots of practice in addressing threats to our business. When automation tools like Buffer and Hootsuite came on the scene, they were sure to make our jobs obsolete and unnecessary. And when Canva became a common tool among the masses, our creative secrets were sure to become commonplace. I wasn't concerned then, and I'm not concerned now for three very simple reasons:

1. I see AI (Artificial Intelligence) as a tool.

2. Tools are only as good as the people who use them.

3. It's our job to become experts in utilizing AI tools so we can better serve our clients.

That's my philosophy with ChatGPT, and I suggest you take the same approach. See how it can make you better and more efficient, but do not use it as a replacement. That would be the opposite of Authentically Social!

Here are some ways to use AI to assist your social media efforts:

- Brainstorming content ideas.

- Coming up with catchy titles for your videos.

- Creating a list of hashtags to help you amplify your content.

- Recommending responses to your posts.

- Helping you craft a perfect response to a positive or negative review.

- Assisting in creating compelling copy for your next social media advertisement.

Remember, while ChatGPT and other AI tools can be helpful for social media management, it's essential to combine its capabilities with human oversight to ensure that content and engagement align with your business's goals and values. (Full disclosure: this section was co-written by ChatGPT.)

Our agency works with a mortgage company out of Iowa and publishes a blog article on their website each week. ChatGPT is a contributor to every blog we write. Our writers start by having ChatGPT help brainstorm topics relevant to that season and the customer demographic we are looking to reach. The topic ideas are run by the client, and together, we choose the one we like best. We then instruct ChatGPT to write a 500-word blog article on the topic with three specific takeaways for the reader. This serves as our rough draft. Next, our team begins to construct the blog article by adding context, personalizing it to our client and their audience, and taking out content that doesn't make sense. All statistics, dates, and other factual information included in the article are validated before publishing. Then, we choose an appropriate image (we may also look for AI assistance here as well) before submitting it to the client for review. The amount we use from ChatGPT varies, but it inevitably helps in every article we write. The more ChatGPT learns our client's voice, the better and more accurate it becomes. Our team loves having a personal assistant at our fingertips, and it enables us to do our job faster and more efficiently.

TAKE ACTION

1. **Choose.** Pick an AI tool or a few AI tools that work for you. As of this writing, ChatGPT is the clear front-runner for market share, but that could change over time. There are many other AI tools that do different things, so research based on your needs.

2. **Decide.** Where do you need assistance? Writing content? Picking images? Adding captions?

3. **Play.** You won't discover the power of AI until you start experimenting with the tools.

Don't let AI overwhelm or intimidate you. You decide whether the information it provides is worthy of being used or not. You can disagree with AI and take your social media post in a completely different direction. It's a brainstorming tool, a first draft, a personal assistant, and you have the final say on what is published on your profiles and what gets left off.

In the World of Social, Done Is Better than Perfect

MANTRA
i know that perfectionism is the enemy of progress.

Some of our agency clients (and my wife) are self-proclaimed perfectionists, and that's a big part of why they're so good at what they do for a living. However, perfectionism can be a "perfect" bottleneck when it comes to getting out digital content consistently. Those who wait to get that perfect video take or write the next New York Times Op-Ed will get passed by those who post (perhaps lower quality) content more frequently. In this case, quantity is actually preferred over quality.

Here today, gone tomorrow.

As mentioned earlier in the book, social media marketing is the long game. Our goal is to stay connected with our audience for as long as it takes until they become customers. This can be weeks or years. A specific article, video, or image will often not even be seen by most of our audience. That's a tough pill to swallow—but often a reality. Therefore, spending too much time and energy on perfection can be detrimental to your ability to stay consistent. You have to find the balance. Don't phone it in or post something you'll later regret—but remind yourself you're human, and humans are flawed. Our content doesn't have to be perfect.

Here are a few ways to stay consistent and avoid perfectionism:

- **Just hit record.** As mentioned in a previous chapter, embrace the one-take challenge by shooting your videos in one-take and being okay with imperfections.

- **Avoid too many cooks in the kitchen.** It's always good to have someone edit your content, but be careful of having too many editors. You may find yourself stuck in revision mode.

- **Set a posting schedule.** Decide on a posting schedule that works for you and your audience. This could be daily, weekly, or monthly, depending on your goals and resources. Stick to your schedule as much as possible to maintain consistency.

- **Use your content calendar.** A content calendar can help you plan and organize your social media content in advance. This can help you stay on track and ensure that you're posting consistently.

- **Batch it.** Organize your content creation by dedicating a specific block of time to creating multiple pieces of content simultaneously. This can help you stay ahead of schedule and ensure that you always have content ready to post.

Recently, I was raving to my wife about an AI video tool I discovered called Vidyo.ai. It automatically selects, edits, and captions top moments from your videos. I thought my audience would love it too, so I went outside to shoot a video about my experience using the tool. Unfortunately, the lighting wasn't great, and I didn't feel my energy was quite there. I could have re-shot the video, but my wife reminded me to take my own advice. It doesn't have to be perfect. It just has to be done. It was good enough—and sometimes good enough is enough. The video ended up resonating very well with my audience and garnered more engagement than any other content that month. It was far from perfect, but performed perfectly!

TAKE ACTION

1. **Embrace the one-take challenge.** Resist the urge to re-record and allow yourself some grace for minor imperfections. Choose to create one video per week or month, and set a goal to stay consistent for at least three months.

2. **Choose one solid editor.** I have one person on my team in charge of helping me avoid looking foolish on my social media. She proofreads everything, and if she says it's okay, I give the okay for the content to go live. More than one person can create a bottleneck for consistency.

3. **If it's not on your calendar, it rarely happens.** To stay consistent with shooting videos or writing content, you need to block it in your calendar. Pick a convenient day and time each week to devote to creating content, and stick to it.

EMBRACE THE ONE TAKE CHALLENGE:
1. Shoot It. 2. Edit It. 3. Post It!

Beyond Your Profile

It is often said that it's much cheaper to retain a customer than to gain a new one. This has certainly been the case in my experience, and I bet for you as well. I view our customers as partners. Their business is an extension of ours. We've underdelivered if they view us as nothing more than a vendor. I encourage my team to find ways to become more than a vendor, and social media has been valuable in helping us achieve that. The next few chapters are principles that focus on how to strengthen relationships with existing customers and bridge the gap between vendor and partner.

4

Keep Your Friends Close, and Your Customers Closer

MANTRA

i won't make the invoice the only time my customers hear from me.

I think it was Chinese general and philosopher Sun Tzu who coined the famous phrase, "Keep your friends close and your enemies closer." I adapted it just a little when thinking about the importance of being connected to your customers. We tend to do a good job connecting with friends and family, but sometimes, we hesitate when it comes to connecting with our business contacts. I understand the hesitation, especially on more personal sites such as Facebook, Instagram, and TikTok. However, I believe the advantages far outweigh the disadvantages. Using these tools to help us build strong and long-lasting relationships with our most valued customers is one of the greatest benefits of social media. Engaging with our customers and their content is a small yet consistent reminder that we see them and that they're important to us. It is my belief that we should be connected to our customers offline and online. Furthermore, if they only hear from us when we need something—or it's invoice time—we may need to rethink our customer engagement strategy.

We're all aware of the standard ways to connect with customers on an ongoing basis. An email, text, phone call, or visit can help keep a relationship strong and healthy. I'm not trying to convince you to stop doing any of those activities. My suggestion is to add social media touch points in addition to your other engagement activities.

Here are some ways to connect with your customers on social media:

- Connect and/or follow them on all appropriate platforms.

- Subscribe to their newsletter.

- Subscribe to their YouTube channel.

- Watch their videos and comment.

- Participate in groups where they're active.

When it comes to staying connected online with customers, don't be afraid to be part of their personal moments, either. In instances like a birthday, anniversary, or other milestone, consider sending personalized messages or greetings to your customers. If they divulge something difficult or challenging, you can be there to share your support. Moments and gestures like these pave the way for a deeper connection between you and your customers on social media.

LET YOUR CUSTOMERS KNOW YOU CARE ABOUT THEM.

SUCCESS STORIES

Like most businesses, the COVID-19 pandemic hit my business pretty hard. In a pretty raw moment, I posted to Facebook about my concern for our business and all that it impacted. I was scared and confused about what moves, if any, I could make. No more than five minutes after I made the post, I received a call from Mike, my business banker. Mike and I were connected on Facebook, and he saw my distressed post. "Corey, things are pretty crazy right now, and I'm here to help," he said. I thought the timing was truly divine intervention, but alas, I later found out it was Facebook. Mike's guidance was such a blessing and helped save my business. I'll never forget it, and Mike has made a friend for life, online and in real life.

TAKE ACTION

1. **Who is Your Inner Circle?** Make a list of your top customers and connect with them on the appropriate platforms.

2. **Set Alerts.** Make the necessary adjustments to ensure you're notified when they post on social media. On LinkedIn, for example, you click a bell icon to get notified.

3. **Schedule Time.** Regularly like, react, and engage with their posts.

4. **Leave Thoughtful Comments.** Take the time to leave a thoughtful and genuine comment on their post. Ask questions, provide compliments, or offer support.

5. **Share Their Content.** If your customers create content that aligns with your brand and is relevant to your audience, share it on your brand's social media. It not only promotes your customers, but also strengthens your relationship with them.

6. **Be There.** Celebrate with them during happy times, and share your support during challenging times.

Be Down with O.P.P.
(Other People's Posts)

MANTRA
i'll never doubt the power
of a digital high-five!

For better or worse, the 90s helped define my musical preferences. One of the many catchy songs that came out of that decade was Naughty By Nature's "O.P.P." and their memorable phrase, "You down with O.P.P.?" Go ahead, feel free to sing the answer—I'll wait. While Treach sang about an entirely different subject, the O.P.P. that I'm referring to in this chapter is **Other People's Posts!** This is one of the most powerful ways to get more results from your efforts on social media.

When we talk about engagement on social media, we often think about how to get more likes, comments, and shares with our own content. Engagement can be just as powerful a tool when applied to the giving of attention to the content of others. By this, I simply mean liking, sharing, and commenting. It's the equivalent of a digital high-five to your connections, and it will mean a great deal to them.

Make it a priority to engage with the content of your customers, prospects, and those that can be a referral source for your business.

Here are just some of the reasons engaging in O.P.P. is critical to your social media success:

- You'll stay "top of mind" with the people who are important to you. It's a subtle way to not let others forget about you.

- Social media sites want you to engage in conversation on their platform, and in doing so, it can have a positive impact on their algorithm. This can result in more visibility of your profile and your content.

- It can mean a lot to people. We all work hard to put out compelling content on our network. It can be a real struggle. When we see a comment or share, it feels good and can go a long way in the value of that relationship.

- Finally, it can act as a gentle reminder that we are waiting for their action on something (a response to an email or a document signature) without actually having to remind them. Often, that email response or DocuSign document magically appears soon thereafter.

Each day, I spend time navigating and reviewing the social media feeds of my clients, customers, and prospects. When I find meaningful and compelling content, I will engage and interact. Sometimes, it may be a like or a share, but mostly, I am very intentional about spending quality time absorbing their content, and will often ask a related question in the comments or add my own comment to strike up meaningful conversation. This is my way of giving them a digital high-five and letting them know that I am invested in them and care about the content they are creating and posting.

If you remember nothing else from this chapter, just be down with O.P.P.! My version, of course.

I'm a big fan of Continuing Education, and I'm eager to learn from other experts in the social media industry. Recently, I heard a fantastic presentation from LinkedIn expert Richard Bliss. He reiterated the importance of engaging with other people's content. Richard made a strong case that the best thing you can do for the visibility of your own profile is to engage in conversations happening on other profiles. Since his talk, I've made an even stronger commitment to leave the comforts of my own platforms and venture out to participate in conversations happening on my connections' profiles. It has resulted in my highest profile views to date, and I've upped my connection requests by 10%.

TAKE ACTION

1. Dedicate 15 minutes per day to engaging in conversation on other people's posts and subsequent comments.

2. Try to avoid one and two word comments like "Amazing," "Great Job," "Fantastic," and instead create thoughtful responses that add to the conversation.

3. When appropriate, ask questions so others can weigh-in and keep the conversation going.

4. Take the last few minutes to check your own profiles and respond to any comments or questions made across your pages.

CONCLUSION

For better or worse, social media has become an integral part of our lives and our businesses. Unfortunately, it's become a place saturated with noise. Businesses that embrace authenticity will stand out as beacons of trust and credibility. Throughout this book, we have explored the transformative power of bringing your authentic self and authentic brand to all areas of your social media marketing.

As the virtual landscape continues to evolve, customers are no longer content with mere transactional exchanges. They want a human connection with the brands they choose to support. Authenticity has become the cornerstone of successful social media strategies, enabling businesses to forge deep, lasting relationships with their audience.

From candid behind-the-scenes glimpses to turning the spotlight on others in our community, the journey toward authenticity requires a willingness to embrace vulnerability and transparency. Being Authentically Social is about showcasing the people behind the brand, our passion for our customers and community, and our genuine care for the needs and aspirations of our audience.

As you become truly Authentically Social, I believe you'll inspire engagement, spark conversations, and cultivate a loyal community that will lead to real business results.

Wait...you're still here?
It's over!
Go back to work.
Go!

ANY FERRIS BUELLER
FANS OUT THERE?

Here are a few bonus principles
that didn't quite fit into the book.

I hope you enjoy.

Beware of the Keyboard Warriors

MANTRA
i will turn my critics
into champions.

If you don't mind waiting 30 minutes to get your food."

"You should have told me before my appointment that your parking lot was full."

"It felt more like a sauna than a hotel lobby."

Ah, yes, the keyboard warrior.

They roam the internet looking for people and small businesses to attack. They tend to always look for the bad in any given situation and will hold it over their entire experience. While they typically won't say anything about their experience to your face, they are notorious for picking the perfect, often hurtful words to hurl at you in their reviews while they are hidden away, safe and sound, in their basement dungeons.

Unfortunately, we live in a world where Keyboard Warriors are quick and eager to leave a negative review when something goes wrong or is unexpected. They feel a moral duty and obligation to let everyone know about this wrong and oftentimes don't look to resolve the situation before they do so. In some cases, their concerns or complaints are warranted but could have easily been handled with communication between them and the seller. This is what many of us find most frustrating about negative reviews. Since today's digital world provides a platform for people to easily share their experiences with your business, good and bad, it is critical and imperative that we always strive to provide our best service and customer experience.

The above description might sound a little dramatic, but if you're a business owner or individual blindsided by a negative post online, this may feel very real to you. The challenge a business can face because of less-than-stellar reviews is painful. Any negative reviews, founded in truth or not, can give future prospects and current clients pause to proceed when they read them. In a perfect world, we'd have nothing but happy, positive experience reviews. However, for most of us, this is not always the case. We can do our best, but sometimes things can and do go wrong. Finding ways to minimize the negative impact on your business and resolving any negative experience one might have will be key to success when battling these Keyboard Warriors.

If you or your business should receive negative feedback online, here are ways I suggest to respond:

- **Don't react immediately or impulsively.** Sleep on it and give it some thought before responding.

- **Bend a little.** Be empathetic and try to fix the issue, even if this means bending a little bit to satisfy your customer.

- **Ask!** If the issue is successfully resolved, ask the reviewer to update or change the review.

- **Let's take this offline.** If you can't fix the issue, take it offline to avoid the back-and-forth for everyone to see.

- **Always respond.** Even if the review is inaccurate or just plain false, be diplomatic, but share the facts so that the public can see.

- **Know When To Fold 'Em.** Don't go to war with a reviewer to the bitter end. It's a battle you can't win. Do your best to find resolve, but know when to step back and walk away from the conversation.

As my wife will tell you, I've been known to impulsively buy something when hit with a good Facebook advertisement—especially during the holidays. Right before Hanukkah, I was scrolling through my feed when up popped this cool-looking toy that I thought would be perfect for my son, Milo. The ad showed a video of a boy and his grandma having the best time of their lives. I was immediately sold! I clicked on the ad, and it directed me to Amazon, where I was met with a myriad of reviews. As I began to skim through them, it was the third one down that caught my attention. I noticed a two-star review was updated to a four-star review. The reviewer wrote about his initial negative experience but noted he needed to update his review after the company reached out, resolved his complaint, and addressed his concern. This action by the company satisfied him so much that he revised his original review. His revision gave me confidence that I would have a good customer service experience, even if something went wrong with my purchase. I felt more comfortable and inclined to make this purchase after considering the outcome of that original review and considering the abundance of other positive reviews that this toy had. Lucky for Milo, because it turned out to be a favorite toy!

People don't expect perfection. They appreciate when businesses are transparent and put effort into fixing a problem. Let's commit to not fearing negative feedback but instead to using it as an opportunity to create trust and credibility in the way we handle that feedback.

TAKE ACTION

- **What is out there?** Do a digital audit of any sites where customers can leave feedback about you or your business.

- **Respond.** Make sure to respond to all positive reviews. People love being thanked for taking the time to write a kind review.

- **See above.** If you should find a negative review, use the guide above to respond accordingly. If it's an old review, you may decide just to leave it alone.

- **Take the reins.** Create a process for collecting positive feedback on your review sites and social media. The more proactive you are in getting positive reviews, the less impact a negative review will have, should it come your way.

You Have to Pay to Play

MANTRA
if i'm using social media for business, i need a budget.

In years past, businesses could build an audience on social media and promote their products or services – all without spending a dime. Those days are long gone, and, except for the rare exceptions, you have to spend money to make money on social media. The question isn't if you should have an advertising budget for social media, but rather, what is the right budget and the best strategy for those dollars?

You may be thinking to yourself, "If I create exceptional content, won't they just come?" While it is important to create great content and make posts that you believe will resonate with your ideal customer, unfortunately, this approach alone isn't enough in today's digital marketplace. For example, a typical post to your Facebook or Instagram business page is only shown to a small fraction of your audience. You must boost the post to increase the percentage of people who see it. I like to use the analogy of a campfire. Your social media post is the small flame, and boosting that post is like adding lighter fluid to the flame. The more you boost, the bigger the flame.

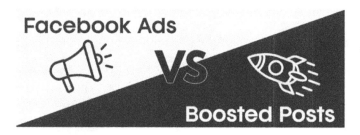

Boosted Post vs. Traditional Ad:

It is important to understand that boosting a post is not the same as running a social media advertisement. Furthermore, it's equally necessary to know when to use each to your advantage. Boosting a post is simply spending money to get more people to see a specific piece of content you posted to social media. A social media ad is more comprehensive and is specifically designed with a target audience, a call to action, and a specific start and finish.

Spending money to boost a post is most effectively done when you want to amplify your existing content to a larger audience. When your goal is to get page engagement with the content you've created, this would be a great time to allocate some money toward a boosted post. On the other hand, if your goal is to build your email list, drive more traffic to your website, or sell a certain seasonal product, your money would be better spent on a traditional social media ad. Knowing your goal and strategy will help guide you in deciding how best to spend your social media advertising budget.

One important thing to note when running an ad on social media is that these platforms like to keep people within the walls of their sites as much as possible. So, if you run an ad campaign that leads people to your website, you can expect to pay a higher cost per click or cost per lead than if you had them fill out a form while remaining on the social platform.

Also, it is important to understand what is a realistic expectation for the call to action within the ad you're creating. Depending on where the person is in the buying cycle, your call to action should be structured around what makes the most sense for that sale to take place. What type of sale are you trying to make? Is it a shorter and fairly inexpensive sale (like a cup of coffee), or is it higher-priced and more complex (e.g., a dental procedure)? Sometimes, the right call to action is one that leads them to more information. A "Learn More" clickable button, email list, or representative through a "Contact Us" link are all calls to actions where they can get to know you and your product better. Larger purchases and longer cycles often require more touches. Your potential prospects may need to see multiple ads and learn more about you in multiple ways. Other purchases may need less explanation and persuasion and may happen quicker using a "Buy Now" call to action.

Whether you run a traditional ad or boosted post, it's imperative that you carefully choose your target audience. By targeting the right demographics (age, gender, likes, and interests), it is more likely to get people seeing your ad who will be your most active prospects.

Lookalike Audiences:

A lookalike audience is a targeting feature used in digital advertising campaigns. It refers to a group of individuals who share similar characteristics, behaviors, or interests with an existing customer base. By using lookalike audiences, social media platforms can help you target specific audiences that you haven't yet reached.

Remarketing:

Remarketing, also known as retargeting, is a digital marketing strategy that involves targeting individuals who have previously interacted with your brand or website. It is a technique used to re-engage potential customers who have shown some level of interest in a product or service but have not yet made a purchase. If you've searched for a product on Amazon and suddenly saw it while navigating your social media newsfeed, then you've been a target of a remarketing ad. It's a great strategy to ensure prospects don't forget about you.

Budget:

Last but not least, let's talk about the ad budget. How much money should you put in each month to get the desired outcome in sales or engagement? The amount you decide will vary depending on the size of your business and the size of the sale you want to make. In general, small businesses tend to spend in the hundreds per month (under $1,000 when getting started). Start by spending in this range to see what results (page likes and engagement) you can get, then adjust as needed. When boosting a post, be sure to spend your money on the posts with the most compelling content. These posts should already have good engagement and just need a match to light the fire.

Social media has become a pay-to-play model for businesses. Knowing the best and most effective way to use those ad dollars will help you see better results.

A few years ago, we worked with a golf apparel company. They asked us to run a social media advertising campaign for a few of their new products. We scheduled the campaigns around major golf events, as we knew more people would be interested during that time. We boosted some of their highest-performing posts to reach a larger number of their followers and ran other ads targeting their largest buying demographic (men between the ages of 40–55). Finally, we ran a remarketing campaign through Facebook and Instagram for people who visited their website and didn't make a purchase. Although these ads kept the company 'top of mind' with prospects, they were still not seeing an increased number of conversions. We monitored email opt-ins, website visits, and product purchases, and determined people were abandoning the website at checkout. We paused the campaign so they could work on the optimization of their website and improve the user experience. Keeping a close eye on the data enabled us to catch the issue quickly and and save their ad budget until fixed issues that were causing potential buyers to not purchase.

1. **Choose the right platform.** Start by choosing the social media platform that is most relevant to your business and target audience. Over the years, our agency has found Facebook and Instagram to be the best platforms for getting results with social media advertising. Other platforms are continuing to build their advertising solutions, so this could change over time.

2. **Define your target audience.** Based on factors such as age, gender, location, interests, and behaviors, you can identify a target audience. This will help you increase the likelihood of people being interested when seeing your ad or boosted post.

3. **Set your budget.** Your social media advertising campaign budget and chosen ad format(s) need to fit your goals. Social media platforms like Facebook and Instagram offer various options, from sponsored posts to carousel ads to video ads.

4. **Create compelling ad content.** Ads need to be visually appealing, engaging, and aligned with your brand's messaging and values. Use high-quality images or videos, clear and concise copy, and a strong call to action to encourage your audience to take action.

5. **Measure your results.** Use the analytics tools provided by the social media platform to track the performance of your ads and adjust your strategy accordingly. Look at metrics such as reach, engagement, click-through rate, and conversion rate to assess the effectiveness of your ads and make data-driven decisions going forward.

PRINCIPLE 23

Turn Cold Calls into Warm Leads

MANTRA
The power is not in my network, it's in my network's network.

I'm often asked why I talk about certain social media sites and not others. The answer is simple. I talk about the sites where our clients have seen results. And I ignore the rest.

Over the past decade, we've seen more appointments made, phones ring, and cash registers ka-ching on LinkedIn than any other platform. It's not for all businesses, but for most of us, LinkedIn is flooded with opportunities and possibilities. And yet, we allow our profiles to collect dust. We neglect our network. And we leave inbox messages unread!

I know what you're thinking, "But Corey, it's so spammy now!" That's true. Beyond Salesy Sales Steve and Auto-Response Anna, there's a plethora of quality prospects waiting to hear from you. You just have to find them and make it easy for them to find you.

When using LinkedIn as a prospecting tool, I always recommend either reaching out to your direct connections or looking for prospects that are a 2nd-degree connection. The true power of LinkedIn is in those 2nd-degree connections. A **2nd-degree connection** means you both have a mutual connection. Explore that connection and see if the mutual "friend" can introduce you. This can turn an otherwise cold outreach into a warm lead prepared to hear from you. The now warm lead has heard from a reliable source that what you have to share could be of value to them. This has worked brilliantly for so many of our clients over the years, who have put this practice into habit. Once you start exploring your 2nd-degree connections, your networking world will truly open to new opportunities.

Here are five additional ways to make sure you're getting the most out of using LinkedIn:

1. **Let LinkedIn know who you know.** If you're not actively connecting to customers and prospects, LinkedIn can't do its job. Spend each of the next four weeks expanding your network by 16 people. Make sure you know them, and you can work together in some capacity. At the end of the month, you'll have 64 new connections and will be off and running.

2. **Update your professional summary.** Make it less of a bio and more of a benefit-rich summary of how you serve others. Think less about you and more about them.

3. **Request three new quality recommendations.** These recommendations should be from recent clients who absolutely loved working with you. They will sing your praises like no one else can. You can repurpose these beyond LinkedIn, and they will be there each time someone visits your profile. Also, consider removing three old recommendations that are either old or not as high quality.

4. **Engage with O.P.P. (Other People's Posts).** Spend 15 minutes a day interacting with your network's content. Give them a like, post a comment, or share a valuable tip to your feed. By engaging in their content, you are supporting them and reminding them how amazing you are at the same time.

5. **Follow company pages.** Whether they are clients or prospects, LinkedIn company pages often give great insights to smart salespeople. Job openings, promotions, and other key company updates are often shared on these pages. You can use this information to get your foot in the door or create new revenue streams with key clients.

Stay consistent with the above action items, and I feel confident that you'll see better results with your LinkedIn prospecting.

Last year, I conducted a Social Selling workshop for a group of Dale Carnegie sales consultants. During a session, I demonstrated the power of looking for 2nd-degree connections when prospecting for new business. Later that week, one of the attendees was looking for an opportunity to do business with United Way. As she explored their company page on LinkedIn, the attendee noticed she had a 2nd degree connection with the Director of Training and Development. That mutual connection happened to be a Dale Carnegie graduate and a huge advocate for the program. The introduction was made, and Dale Carnegie has had a great relationship with United Way ever since. That's the power of the 2nd-degree connection!

1. Start by making sure you've connected with your network. You should easily have over 500+ connections on LinkedIn.

2. Come up with a targeted list of companies or individuals you'd like to work with and write them down.

3. Do a search on LinkedIn and look for individuals with a #2 near their name. This indicates you have a mutual connection.

4. Explore that mutual connection, and see if you have enough of a relationship that would warrant an introduction to this prospect.

5. Request the introduction by using LinkedIn's get introduced feature or simply send a message.

6. Determine if an introduction makes sense based on the strength of your mutual connection's relationship with the prospect.

7. If appropriate, ask for an introduction via LinkedIn or email, and watch the magic happen!

OK, that's really it.

But before I let you go, I wanted to make sure you know where to find me and how to access other social media insights.

LinkedIn

This is my #1 spot on social media. I love engaging with other business professionals, giving appreciation to clients who have hired me, and sharing my thoughts on being Authentically Social.

Corey Perlman, CSP (Certified Speaking Professional)

Keynote Speaker and Executive Consultant on the topics of Social Media and Digital Marketing

Instagram

This is where I share more behind-the-scenes footage of speaking events and short video tips and tricks. Instagram.com/CoreyPerlmanSpeaks

YouTube

This is where you'll find speaking clips, training videos, podcasts, and more. If you want the deep dive, YouTube is where you'll find the treasure! Go to: YouTube.com/CoreyPerlman

I look forward to watching you and your business become Authentically Social! I truly believe people want to connect with people, and the more you look to help and serve, the more business will come your way.

About the Author

(Written by Talia Perlman, age 13 and Milo Perlman, age 9)

Corey Perlman is a professional speaker. He has two kids named Talia and Milo. He also has a dog, Domino, and his lovely wife and business partner, Jessica. Corey's son and daughter play lacrosse and love swimming in the pool and lake. Jessica is an introvert who loves reading and meditating. He goes on a lot of trips, and people actually like listening to him. We get to sign books with him from time to time. He is the boss of some people, and we see them on his computer sometimes. They spend a lot of time talking about Instagram and other stuff.

Our dad does a podcast with Poppo about being a Nurturing Father. This program helps dads become the best fathers they can be for their children. Our dad is a nurturing father … most of the time.

He already has two books, and you are reading his third! He promised to jump in the lake with us if it becomes a bestseller, so please tell your friends!

Thanks,
Talia Perlman and Milo Perlman

www.ingramcontent.com/pod-product-compliance
Lightning Source LLC
Chambersburg PA
CBHW071001050326
40689CB00014B/3450